THE LMS REMEMBERED

Plate 1 A mixture of pre-grouping and post-grouping locomotives; an LMS built 2P 4-4-0 No. 654 attached to a Bowen-Cooke LNWR 'Prince of Wales' class 4-6-0 coming off shed at Crewe on 7th April 1934. *F.G. Carrier*

Overleaf: *Plate 2* All out effort from Kirtley rebuilt Johnson single framed Midland 1P No. 84 piloting an LMS built 4F 0-6-0 out of Great Rocks Tunnel on a down freight. No. 84 was a Rowsley engine and would have been attached at Rowsley for the climb to Peak Forest.

84
Nº 86
GREAT ROCKS
TUNNEL
161 YARDS

THE LMS REMEMBERED

by

J.S. WHITELEY and G.W. MORRISON

Oxford Publishing Co. Oxford

SBN 86093 030 0

Plate 3 A Johnson Midland 2P 4-4-0 built 1882-1883 and as subsequently rebuilt by Deeley. No. 338 is seen fitted with a Belpaire firebox and extended smokebox heading a down train between Little Eaton Junction and Peckwash Mill sidings, north of Derby.

F.G. Carrier

ACKNOWLEDGMENT

The authors would like to express their gratitude and appreciation to all the photographers who have so kindly allowed them to use their work and for the friendly assistance offered by so many during the preparation of this book. Particular thanks are offered to Mike Carrier for allowing inclusion of so many of his Father's hitherto unpublished pictures and to Margaret Morley for her part in typing the manuscript.

Typesetting by Gem Graphic Services, Didcot, Oxon.

Printed by Blackwell's in the City of Oxford.

Published by Oxford Publishing Co.
8 The Roundway,
Headington,
Oxford.

Contents

Introduction

On January 1st 1923 the London Midland & Scottish Railway came into being as the largest of the 'Big Four' companies which were created by the grouping of Britain's railways by Act of Parliament. Almost 10,500 locomotives were inherited by the LMS at the grouping and the principal constituents in alphabetical order were the Caledonian Railway, the Furness Railway, the Glasgow & South Western Railway, the Highland Railway, the London and North Western Railway (including the North London Railway which had been worked by the LNWR from 1909), the Midland Railway (including the London Tilbury & Southend Railway which had been absorbed by the MR in 1912) and the North Staffordshire Railway. One notable exception from the above is the Lancashire & Yorkshire Railway which had in fact amalgamated with the LNWR exactly one year before the grouping.

By far the greatest contribution in terms of numbers and also advanced passenger locomotive designs came from the LNWR It is, therefore, easy to understand why there was such bad feeling when the MR became the dominating partner in the London Midland & Scottish group when the best they could offer was a variety of 4-4-0s for express passenger work which were certainly no match for the 'Prince of Wales' and 'Claughton' 4-6-0s of the LNWR.

Things did not improve when Sir Henry Fowler, who had been CME of the MR since 1909, succeeded George Hughes as CME of the LMS in 1925 and perpetuated the MR small engine policy. Only in 1927 did the arrival of the 'Royal Scot' 4-6-0s herald the introduction of some new larger locomotives. The Midland stranglehold on the LMS did not really end until William Stanier (later Sir William Stanier) arrived from Swindon and was appointed CME of the LMS in 1932. This in turn heralded massive withdrawals of pre-grouping locomotives which were being replaced by more efficient modern designs which lasted until steam was withdrawn from BR in 1968.

This book is an attempt to show a balanced selection of locomotive designs, some of which were inherited by the LMS in 1923, the remainder of which were conceived by the LMS during its twenty-five years existence until Britain's railways were Nationalised on January 1st 1948.

J.S. Whiteley
Jan. 1979

Plate 4 Above Kirtley double framed Midland 1P 2-4-0, usually referred to as the '800' class due to the original numbers of the first engines being 800 - 829. Forty-eight of these engines were built 1870-1871 but only twenty-four were in service at the grouping, the last one being withdrawn in 1936. No. 67 is seen here at Nottingham Midland.

F.G. Carrier

Plate 5 Above Johnson Midland 1P 2-4-0 No. 238 heading a down local train from Derby near Little Eaton Junction. Sixty-five of these engines were built 1876-1881 and most were re-built with Belpaire fireboxes from 1926 onwards. One engine survived nationalisation and was withdrawn in 1949.

F.G. Carrier

Plate 6 Left One of the Johnson/ Deeley Somerset & Dorset Joint Railway 2P 4-4-0s built 1903-1914. No. 323 is seen fitted with an exhaust smoke injector and being inspected closely by a young admirer. The five engines in this class were rebuilt by Fowler in 1921 similar to the Midland '483' class and absorbed in LMS stock in 1930. No. 323 is about to leave Cromford on a down train in the early 1930's.

F.G. Carrier

Plate 7 Above Rebuilt Johnson Midland 2P 4-4-0 No. 442 with attractive combined sweeping splashers leaving Derby on an up train, passing London Road Junction. Fifty-five of these 6 ft 6 in engines were built 1893-1900 and all the class was rebuilt by Deeley from 1905. Fowler rebuilt thirty-five from 1914 onwards (excluding No. 442) to conform with his '483' class.

F.G. Carrier

Plate 8 Below Johnson Midland 2P '483' class 4-4-0 No. 443 with bogie brakes, on a most attractive rake of stock overtakes a double-headed freight at Breadsall Crossing whilst heading a down express. These engines were built 1882-1901, rebuilt by Deeley from 1904 and further rebuilt with superheater etc. by Fowler between 1912-1923. They were the final development of the Midland Class 2 4-4-0s.

F.G. Carrier

Plate 9 Above A BR scene at Stamford Town on 23rd July 1952. Johnson Midland 2P 4-4-0 No. 40543 is seen leaving with the 12.40 Peterborough-Leicester with No. 40559 alongside whilst yard shunting.

P.H. Wells

Plate 10 Above Johnson Midland 3P 4-4-0 No. 725 about to depart from Nottingham Midland with a Lincoln train on 23rd May 1939. Eighty of these 6 ft 9 in engines were built between 1900 and 1905 and No. 725 is seen here as rebuilt by Fowler with larger cylinders and superheater.

J.P. Wilson

Plate 11 Left Another rebuilt 3P 4-4-0 No. 722 heading a Nottingham-Lincoln train near Colwick Level Crossing in March 1933.

J.P. Wilson

Plate 12 Above One of the two hundred and five Johnson Midland 1P 0-4-4Ts No. 58065 (formerly LMS No. 1367) leaving Southwell with a push and pull train to Rolleston Junction on 29th July 1958. Some of these engines had 5 ft 7 in driving wheels but this is one of the 5 ft 4 in engines as rebuilt from 1925 with Belpaire firebox.
Peter Groom

Plate 13 Right Sister engine 58066 (LMS No. 1368) is seen at Oxenhope with a local train from Keighley about 1955.
W.H. Foster

Plate 14 Left Twenty-eight of these Johnson 0-4-0 Saddletanks were built between 1883 and 1903, some with 13 in x 20 in cylinders and some with 15 in x 20 in cylinders. Twenty-three engines were in service at the grouping, four survived nationalisation and the last was withdrawn from service in 1958. No. 1509 is seen at Derby.

F.G. Carrier

Plate 15 Right Johnson Midland 1F 0-6-0T seen at Skipton in 1950. Two hundred and eighty of these engines were introduced from 1874 and many were rebuilt with Belpaire fireboxes from 1919 onwards. No. 41666, however, is seen with non-Belpaire boiler and safety valve on the dome.

W.H. Foster

Plate 16 Left No. 41708 of the same class but with a different cab and Belpaire boiler as seen at Staveley on 9th May 1964. This engine has fortunately been preserved.

G.W. Morrison

Plate 17 Right Only eight of these Adams and Hookham North Stafford 0-6-4Ts were built between 1916 and 1919. They were the NSR Class F and No. 2053 is seen at Derby. The last engine was withdrawn from service in 1936.

A.G. Ellis Collection

Plate 18 Right Whitelegg London, Tilbury and Southend 4-4-2T No. 2111 which was actually constructed subsequent to the grouping in 1923 seen on a Southend train.

A.G. Ellis Collection

Plate 19 Below One of the eight Whitelegg London, Tilbury and Southend 'Baltic' tanks at St. Albans in 1930. They were built in 1912 and were the first 4-6-4 tank engines in Britain. This engine was originally numbered 2106 and the last engine in this class was withdrawn in 1934.

A.G. Ellis Collection

Plate 20 Right London, Tilbury and Southend 3P 4-4-2T is seen with a full head of steam on a Fenchurch Street via Upminster train.

A.G. Ellis Collection

Plate 21 Above Kirtley Midland double framed 1F 0-6-0 No. 2592 working hard on a down freight near Cromford. Four hundred and seventy of these engines were built from 1863 and this engine is seen as originally built with Salter spring balance safety valves on the dome. The last engine was withdrawn from service in 1951.

F.G. Carrier

Plate 22 Below One of the Kirtley Midland double framed 0-6-0s with Class 2 boiler and Ramsbottom safety valves in place of the original Salter valves.

F.G. Carrier

Plate 23 Right Johnson Midland 2F 0-6-0 with 4 ft 11 in wheels. Nine hundred and thirty-five of these engines were built between 1875 and 1908 and No. 3153 is seen here with Belpaire firebox at Derby.
F.G. Carrier

Plate 24 Above No. 43814 is seen after nationalisation with a freight at Cheadle Heath with a Class 3 Belpaire boiler.
T. Lewis

Plate 25 Right One hundred and ninety-two Fowler Midland 4F 0-6-0s were built between 1911 and 1922 and No. 3951 which was built for the Midland by Armstrong-Whitworth is seen on a down rake of empty wagons near Breadsall Crossing. The housings for tail rods can clearly be seen on the buffer beam and these were later removed and the holes blanked off. The beading on the splashers was a feature of these Midland built 0-6-0s.
F.G. Carrier

Plate 26 Left An unidentified Webb LNWR 'Precedent' class 1P 2-4-0 with pre-grouping number is seen just after the grouping on an up train believed to be just south of Tamworth. One hundred and sixty-six of these 6 ft 9 in engines were built between 1874 and 1901.

F.G. Carrier

Plate 28 Below Whale LNWR 'Precursor' 4-4-0 No. 25245 *Antaeus* at Shugborough Park on a down local on 11th August 1939. (See also *Plate 240*).

E.G. Ashton

Plate 27 Above Webb 'Precedent' No. 5000 *Princess Beatrice* stands at Nottingham Low Level with a Northampton train.

T.G. Hepburn

Plate 29 Below Rebuilt 'Precursor' No. 25304 *Greyhound* with superheater and Belpaire firebox stands at Bletchley on an Oxford train in 1938.

C.R.L. Coles

Plate 30 Right Bowen-Cooke 'George the Fifth' class 4-4-0 No. 5343 *Otterhound* which was built in May 1911. This class of ninety engines was a development of the 'Precursor' 4-4-0s and were built at Crewe between 1910 and 1915. Only three engines survived nationalisation, the last one being withdrawn in 1948.

F.G. Carrier

Plate 31 Left Bowen-Cooke 'Prince of Wales' Class 3P 4-6-0 No. 25791 on a very mixed freight at South Kenton. Two hundred and forty-five of these engines were constructed between 1911 and 1921 with one additional engine constructed after the grouping in 1924. 20,000 were added to their numbers in 1934 and many of the latter survivors were rebuilt with Belpaire fireboxes as seen here.

A.G. Ellis Collection

Plate 32 Right Another 'Prince of Wales' rebuilt with a Belpaire firebox, No. 25818 is seen on an up local at Shugborough Park on 11th August 1939.

E.G. Ashton

Plate 33 Above The Bowen-Cooke 'Claughton' four cylinder 4-6-0s were surely the pride of LNWR. One hundred and thirty of these fine engines were built at Crewe between 1913 and 1921 and here No. 5984, paired with a Robinson ROD tender is approaching Duffield on a down Manchester express.

F.G. Carrier

Plate 34 Below Another 'Claughton' 4-6-0 No. 5903 *Duke of Sutherland* (named after a director of the LNWR) is heading an up express near Tamworth.

F.G. Carrier

Plate 35 Right From 1928 the LMS rebuilt twenty 'Claughtons' with larger boilers. These were later fitted with smoke deflectors and No. 6004 is seen heading a down freight on Dillicar Troughs in 1946. This was the last engine of the Class to remain in service, being formerly named *Princess Louise.* It was finally withdrawn from service in 1948 having outlasted the previous member of the Class by about seven years.
W. Philip Conolly

Plate 36 Left A Webb LNWR 1P 2-4-2T No. 6732 in immaculate condition. One hundred and sixty of these 5 ft 6 in engines were built between 1890 and 1897 and the last one survived until 1955.
A.G. Ellis Collection

Plate 37 Right The slightly heavier 5 ft 0 in Webb LNWR 1P 0-6-2T is seen here. Eighty of these engines were built between 1898 and 1902. Three were withdrawn from service before the grouping and the last was withdrawn in 1953.
F.G. Carrier

Plate 38 Left Webb LNWR 'Cauliflower' 0-6-0 No. 8589 on a local near Keswick. Three hundred and ten of these engines were built between 1880 and 1902 and this was one of the latter survivors, being rebuilt with a Belpaire firebox.

E.E. Smith

Plate 39 Right Another rebuilt 'Cauliflower' No. 8422 is seen on a three coach train near Keswick. Sixty-nine of these engines survived until nationalisation.

E.E. Smith

Plate 40 Below A Whale '19 in Goods' Class 4F 4-6-0 No. 8843 heading a down train has just emerged from Milford Tunnel shortly after leaving Duffield. One hundred and seventy of these engines were built between 1906 and 1909 many being fitted with Belpaire fireboxes in later years. Only three survived nationalisation, the last one being withdrawn in 1950.

F.G. Carrier

Plate 41 Above Bowen-Cooke LNWR 7F Class 'G2a' No. 49340 climbing Grayrigg Bank with a down freight in April 1954.

W.H. Foster

Plate 42 Below Only four of these Pettigrew Furness 6 ft 6 in 4-4-0s were built between 1900 and 1901, the last engine being withdrawn in 1931. No. 10144 is seen leaving Carlisle believed to be on a Maryport train.

A.G. Ellis Collection

Plate 43 Above An Aspinall 2P 4-4-2 (L & YR Class L1) in full cry seen in its final form with wide chimney and circular smoke box on saddle. Forty of these 'high flyer' Atlantics were built between 1899 and 1902 with massive 7 ft 3 in driving wheels. All were in service at the grouping and the last one was withdrawn in 1934.

A.G. Ellis Collection

Plate 44 Right Sister engine No. 10307 picks up water on Salwick troughs in August 1930 with a Blackpool Central-Skipton train. These engines were never superheated and were the only inside cylinder Atlantics in Britain with the exception of one unique GWR 4-4-2.

F. Dean

Plate 45 Left Another 7 ft 3 in Atlantic No. 10336 is seen leaving Ansdell in October 1926 with an afternoon Liverpool Exchange-Blackpool Central train.

F. Dean

Plate 46 Above Hughes L & YR 5P 4-6-0 No. 10438 on Lea Road troughs with a return Blackpool excursion overtaking a 4F 0-6-0 also on a return excursion. No. 10438 was one of the engines which entered service early in 1923, the first engines of this class appearing in 1921 (see also *Plate 248*).

A.G. Ellis Collection

Plate 47 Above Only one of these Hughes 4-6-0s survived long enough to carry its BR number and it is seen here as No. 50455 passing Burton Salmon on a Blackpool-York special on 1st July 1951.

P.H. Wells

Plate 48 Left Hughes L & YR Rail Motor No. 10606 at Agecroft. Eighteen of these were built between 1906 and 1911, the last unit being withdrawn shortly after nationalisation in 1948.

A.G. Ellis Collection

Plate 49 Right Aspinall L & YR 2-4-2T No. 10869 passes Holbeck with a down local. These were the L & YR Class K2 engines, 309 of which were built between 1889 and 1910.

A.G. Ellis Collection

Plate 50 Below Late in its life No. 50646 is seen running into Bamford with the 09.00 Hope–Sheffield local on 28th September 1955.

R.E. Vincent

Plate 51 Right On 26th May 1956 No. 50865 fitted with extended bunker is seen heading a Calder Valley local passing Heaton Lodge Junction, Mirfield.

B.R. Goodlad

Plate 52 Right Hughes L & YR 4-6-4T, No 11113 leaving Ansdell in July 1927 with a Manchester Victoria-Blackpool Central train. These engines were not built until 1924 but were essentially a Lancashire and Yorkshire design being Class P1. These were the tank engine version of the Hughes 4-6-0 and all ten were withdrawn between 1938 and 1942.

F. Dean

Plate 53 Left The massive proportions of these 6 ft 3 in four cylinder 'Baltic' tanks can be seen in this side view of No. 11117.

A.G. Ellis Collection

Plate 54 Below The Aspinall L & YR 2F 0-6-0s were a Class of 448 being built between 1889 and 1917 (L & YR Class F19). Some of these engines were later rebuilt with Belpaire fireboxes but No. 52362 is seen as originally built heading a special goods near Leyland in 1949.

W.H. Foster

Plate 55 Above McIntosh Caledonian 'Dunalastair IV' with non-superheated boiler. Nineteen of these engines were built between 1904 and 1910 the last one surviving until 1948.
A.G. Ellis Collection

Plate 56 Right Drummond built twenty 'Small Ben' Class 2P 4-4-0s for the Highland Railway between 1898 and 1906. No. 14401 *Ben Vrackie* is seen still with smokebox wingplates shunting at Inverness on 22nd August 1928.
E.G. Ashton

Plate 57 Below The smokebox wingplates have been removed in this picture of Nos. 14402 *Ben Armin* and 14408 *Ben Hope* seen leaving Keith.
A.G. Ellis Collection

Plate 58 Left The 'Large Ben' 2P 4-4-0s were built by Drummond for the Highland Railway between 1908 and 1909. Only six of these engines were built and No. 14417 *Ben na Caillach* is seen fitted with extended smokebox at Aviemore on 15th April 1933.
F.G. Carrier

Plate 59 Right Pickersgill Caledonian 3P 4-4-0 is seen here with its BR No. 54494 at Perth with a train from Dundee. These were the Pickersgill '72' class.
T.G. Hepburn

Plate 60 Left Sister engine No. 14501 in LMS days at Perth on 21st May 1933. All forty-eight of these engines carried their BR numbers 54461-54508, the first one being withdrawn in 1953 and the last one ten years later.
F.G. Carrier

Plate 61 Left Ten of these McIntosh Caledonian '908' Class 4P 4-6-0s were built in 1906, mainly for use on the Clyde coast line. Nos. 14610 and 14612 were originally named *Sir James King* and *Barochan* but these names were removed shortly after the grouping. No. 14616 is seen here on a northbound freight shortly after leaving Perth in the early 1930's .

A.G. Ellis Collection

Plate 62 Above The Drummond Highland Railway 3P 'Castle' 4-6-0s were built between 1900 and 1917 in three separate batches by Dübs & Co and NBL. A total of nineteen were built, sixteen with 5 ft 9 in driving wheels and the last three, Nos. 14691/3 with 6 ft 0 in driving wheels. Here we see one of the three 6 ft 0 in engines No. 14692 *Darnaway Castle* leaving Inverness.

A.G. Ellis Collection

Plate 63 Left 'River' class 4-6-0 No. 14757, formerly HR No. 71 *River Spey,* standing at Perth shed. Six of these engines were designed by Smith for the HR in 1915 but after they were found to be too heavy for the lines of the HR they were sold to the Caledonian Railway and subsequently proved to be probably their best 4-6-0s.

T.G. Hepburn

'ate 64 Right 'River'
ass 4-6-0 No. 14761
en leaving Carlisle on
northbound freight.
A.G. Ellis Collection

Plate 65 Left McIntosh Caledonian 2P 0-4-4T No. 55204 shunting on the docks of Oban in the summer of 1961. There were sixty-eight of these CR '439' class engines built between 1900 and 1914, the majority survived to Nationalisation, the last one being withdrawn in 1962. In later years many were fitted with these ugly stove pipe chimneys.
J.S. Whiteley

Plate 66 Right One of the twelve Pickersgill Caledonian '944' class 4P 4-6-2Ts No. 15351 seen on a Glasgow suburban train. They were built in 1917 and the last engines of the class ended their days as banking engines at Beattock.
A.G. Ellis Collection

Plate 67 Left Whitelegg G & SWR 5P 4-6-4T No. 15402 leaving Glasgow St. Enoch on a suburban train of six wheelers. Only six of these splendid engines were built just prior to the grouping, in 1922, and the last one was withdrawn in 1935.
A.G. Ellis Collection

LMS DESIGNS

Plate 68 Above A Fowler 2-6-2T No. 40060 fitted for push and pull working leaving Kensal Green Tunnel on a down empty stock train on 20th June 1959. Seventy of these engines were built between 1930 and 1932 nineteen of which were fitted with condensing apparatus for working to Moorgate.

Peter Groom

Plate 69 Above No. 40061 of the same class and also fitted with push and pull apparatus seen between duties.

Author's Collection

Plate 70 Left These engines were not a particularly good design and after the War most of the Class were fitted with a larger blastpipe and chimney and outside steampipes in an attempt to improve their performance. No. 40047 is seen as modified on 21st March 1954 on empty stock at Willesden.

P.H. Wells

Plate 71 Above In 1935 the Stanier development of the 1930 Fowler design was introduced with a taper boiler with the same basic dimensions. A total of 139 were built at Derby and Crewe between 1935 and 1938 and here No. 40082 is seen fitted with a larger diameter chimney used in conjunction with the 'Adams Vortex' blastpipe. It is seen in July 1959 near Altofts on a Leeds-Sheffield train.

N. Stead

Plate 72 Below Class 2P 4-4-0 No. 40666 leaving Saltcoates near Ardrossan on 27th July 1959. One hundred and thirty-eight of these engines were built between 1928 and 1932 and were a development of the Midland design with modified dimensions and boiler mountings. All these engines had left-hand drive and they operated over most parts of the LMS System.

G.W. Morrison

Plate 73 Above Three-cylinder compound 4P 4-4-0 No. 40929 heading a Nottingham-Aintree Grand National special near Hazel Grove on 7th April 1951. One hundred and ninety-five of these engines were built between 1924 and 1932 and they were a Fowler post-grouping development of the Midland design.

T. Lewis

Plate 74 Left A down Morecambe train as seen in 1937 near Bell Busk behind 4P 4-4-0 No. 931 which was built by the Vulcan Foundry in 1927.

W.H. Foster

Plate 75 Above Three Compounds for the price of one at Sheffield Midland on August Bank Holiday Saturday 1952. No. 41191 is standing on the platform whilst No. 41119 piloting 41181 pass on the centre road.

B.R. Goodlad

Plate 76 Below Holbeck Compound No. 41137 makes an impressive departure from Leeds City on an up local.

L. Overend

Plate 77 Above Stanier 2P 0-4-4T No. 41900 is seen standing at Ashchurch.

J.D. Edwards

Plate 78 Below What a difference a chimney can make: No. 6408 (BR re-numbered 41908) is seen on a Watford - St. Albans train. Ten engines of this class were introduced in 1932 and credited to Stanier simply because it was a coincidence that they were constructed shortly after Stanier had taken up office, although designed previously by E.G.H. Lemon.

F.G. Carrier

Plate 79 Right A picture taken at St. Pancras in 1936 showing on the left a Fowler 2-6-4T No. 2341 which was Derby built in 1929 and on the right a Fowler 2-6-2T No. 28 which was also built at Derby in 1931 and fitted with condensing apparatus for working to Moorgate.
W. Philip Conolly

Plate 80 Below Fowler 2-6-4T No. 42393 stands at Chester Northgate on 18th May 1959. The last of this class was withdrawn from service in 1966.
S.D. Wainwright

Plate 81 Below Fowler 2-6-4T No. 42339 accelerating from Melton Mowbray (Town) with the 13.45 local to Nottingham in April 1957.
Peter Groom

Plate 82 Above Fowler 2-6-4T No. 42398 on an up local drifting into Heaton Norris alongside LNW G2a Class 0-8-0 No. 49355.

T. Lewis

Plate 84 Below One of the Fairburn 2-6-4Ts introduced in 1945. No. 42680 is seen leaving Mill Hill and Broadway with the 16.40 St. Pancras-St. Albans stopper in May 1957.

B. Morrison

Plate 83 Below Thirty-seven of these three cylinder 2-6-4Ts were built at Derby in 1934 for use on the Southend line. No. 42534 is seen on a down Tilbury Line suburban between Purfleet and Grays on 6th April 1957.

R.E. Vincent

Plate 85 Above Hughes/Fowler mixed traffic 2-6-0s Nos. 13103 and 13101 north of Dunkeld heading the 15.45 Inverness-Glasgow express early in the 1930's. Two hundred and forty-five of these engines were built between 1926 and 1932, ten of which were allocated to the Highland section early in their working lives.
F.G. Carrier

Plate 86 Right These engines were nick-named 'Crabs' and No. 42920 is seen at Nottingham Victoria on 9th May 1964 shunting stock on transfer to the Midland route.
T. Boustead

Plate 87 Left 'Crab' No. 42821 is seen leaving Chester General on a North Wales train on 28th March 1959.
S.D. Wainwright

Plate 88 Above No. 42758 accelerates away from Manchester Exchange on 8th August 1962.
J.S. Whiteley

Plate 89 Left 'Crab' No. 42726 nears the summit at Ais Gill on an up fitted freight.
G.W. Morrison

Plate 90 Above Only forty of these Stanier 2-6-0s were built between 1933 and 1934 at Crewe and No. 42959 is climbing past Thrimby Grange on an early morning up freight on 21st August 1964.

J.S. Whiteley

Plate 91 Left Another member of the Class, No. 42964 is on a Leeds–Manchester local passing Farnley Junction MPD on 17th May 1960.

G.W. Morrison

Plate 92 Above LMS built 4F No. 4153 which was one of the first batches built with right-hand drive, is seen on down mixed freight soon after leaving Derby. These engines were a development of the Midland design and 575 were built by the LMS between 1924 and 1928.

F.G. Carrier

Plate 93 Below 4F No. 44335 heads a down coal train past Wortley Junction, Leeds, on 18th December 1962.

J.S. Whiteley

Plate 94 Above The 4Fs were often seen on passenger workings and here No. 44273 makes a somewhat smokey departure from Kings Lynn in July 1959 with a Hunstanton train.
N. Stead

Plate 95 Below The Stanier Class 5 4-6-0s were possibly the most successful of Stanier's designs with as many as 842 being built between 1935 and 1947. Here No. 45444 with banking assistance climbs past Shap Wells with a mixed freight on 7th October 1967.
J.S. Whiteley

Plate 96 Above Crewe South Class 5 No. 45067 thunders through Bangor with the relief 'Irish Mail' in summer 1963.

B. Wynne

Plate 97 Below A bird's eye view of Bangor on 27th June 1956 with three Class 5s in evidence. The MPD is in the centre of the picture and the goods depot can be seen on the right hand side.

R.E. Vincent

Plate 98 *Above* Simultaneous departures from Bradford Exchange at 08.20 on Saturday 22nd July 1963, No. 44662 on the right hand side is on a Skegness train and No. 44694 on the left is heading a Bridlington train.

D.J. Wood

Plate 99 *Left* The Stanier Class 5s wandered far and wide and No. 44836 is seen leaving Bristol Temple Meads on a holiday extra to Weston-super-Mare on 2nd June 1963.

J.S. Whiteley

Plate 100 *Right* Class 5s or 'Black Fives' as they were often referred to were regularly to be seen on freight duties and early one stormy morning No. 45025 slows at Tebay for banking assistance to Shap Summit on a down mixed freight.

W. Philip Conolly

Plate 101 Above In 1930 two four-cylinder re-boilered 'Claughtons', Nos. 5902 and 5971, were rebuilt at Derby to a design similar to the three-cylinder 'Royal Scot' class 4-6-0s, but with a lower axle loading. In fact very little of the 'Claughtons' was retained and they were quickly nicknamed 'Baby Scots'. No. 5971, as yet unnamed, was the first of these two engines to appear and it is seen here near Bingley on an up express before being fitted with smoke deflectors. This engine was renumbered 5500 in 1934 and given the name *Patriot* in 1937 from a withdrawn 'Claughton', the whole class being subsequently officially described as the 'Patriot' class.

W.H. Foster

Plate 102 Below A further forty 'rebuilds' appeared in 1932 and 1933 from Crewe and Derby although it is very doubtful if any of the original 'Claughton' parts were retained. One of these engines as BR renumbered 45511 *Isle of Man* is passing through Penrith heading an up freight.

W. Philip Conolly

Plate 103 Above The last regular passenger workings of the 'Patriots' were between Leeds and Carnforth and No. 45543 *Home Guard* of Carnforth MPD is leaving Leeds on 6th June 1962 on the 13.54 to Carnforth.
G.W. Morrison

Plate 104 Right An interesting scene at Chester General on 4th March 1961. No. 45547, one of the 'Patriots' never to receive a name, is seen coupled up to 'Hall' class 4-6-0 No. 6922 *Burton Hall* waiting to proceed to 6A shed. Pacific No. 46209 *Princess Beatrice* is seen in the background heading a Holyhead-London meat train.
S.D. Wainwright

Plate 105 Above Eighteen of the class of fifty-two 'Patriots' were rebuilt from 1946 with the same Crewe 2A boiler which had been fitted to the converted 'Royal Scots' (see *Plates 121-4*). They were also fitted with a new Stanier cab and 4000 gallon, nine ton high curved tender. Despite a slightly lower tractive effort these rebuilt 'Patriots' were considered equal to the converted 'Royal Scots' and No. 45530 *Sir Frank Ree* is heading an up Manchester express near Adlington.

T. Lewis

Plate 106 Below No. 45530 *Sir Frank Ree* is leaving Euston during rebuilding of the terminal on 20th May 1964 with the 17.27 semi-fast to Rugby. This was the last of the rebuilt 'Patriots' to be withdrawn in January 1966.

M. Welch

Plate 107 Right Between 1934 and 1936 one hundred and ninety-one three-cylinder 'Jubilee' Class 4-6-0s were built by Stanier for intermediate main line passenger work. They were essentially a taper-boiler development of the Fowler parallel-boilered 'Patriots', and here No. 5614 *Leeward Islands* of Kentish Town is standing at St. Pancras in 1937 paired with the high sided version of the narrow Fowler tender.

F.G. Carrier

Plate 108 Right In 1949 No. 45675 *Hardy* fitted with a Stanier tender is leaving Elstree Tunnel with a down express.

J.G. Dewing

Plate 109 Left No. 45601 *British Guiana* of Camden, with a 2-6-4T banking, starts the two mile climb at 1 in 100 at Macclesfield with the midday Manchester–Euston express in 1957.

M. Welch

Plate 110 Below On the evening of 8th June 1964 No. 45653 *Barham* takes the West Coast main line out of Preston with a down express.

D.I. Wood

Plate 111 Above No. 45606 *Falkland Islands* accelerating away from Bingley towards Keighley on a Leeds–Morecambe train.

W.H. Foster

Plate 112 Below The 'Jubilees' ended their day working from Holbeck MPD, Leeds and No. 45593 *Kolhapur* seen here was one of the last engines to be withdrawn from service, and subsequently preserved. On 12th August 1967 during its Indian summer it is seen nearing Gargrave with the afternoon relief to the down 'Thames-Clyde Express'.

J.S. Whiteley

Plate 113 Above The introduction of the Fowler three-cylinder 'Royal Scot' class 4-6-0s in 1927 made a vast improvement to the express passenger power of the LMSR. The first batch of fifty were all built by North British in 1927 and they proved so successful that a further twenty were built at Derby in 1930. No. 6110 *Grenadier Guardsman,* fitted with bogie brakes which were removed by Stanier, leaves Rugby with a Euston–Glasgow train.

T.G. Hepburn

Plate 114 Left By 1932 all the 'Royal Scots' had been fitted with smoke deflectors and No. 6151 *The Royal Horse Guardsman* is seen fitted with the first type of vertical deflectors at Lancaster Castle but still paired with the original Fowler tender.

W.H. Foster

Plate 115 Below Stanier was responsible for substituting new high sided curved top tenders for the original Fowler tenders and No. 6109 *Royal Engineer* is seen at Tring in 1939, so fitted, heading a down Manchester express. It has also been fitted with angled top smoke deflectors.

C.R.L. Coles

Plate 116 Above No. 46165 *The Ranger (12th London Regt.)* rushes through Watford Junction on a down express.
N. Stead

Plate 117 Below No. 46156 *The South Wales Borderer* in early BR lined black livery is heading a Fleetwood-London fish train near Farrington in 1956.
W.H. Foster

Plate 118 Left Twenty-eight of the 'Royal Scots' were still running with Fowler parallel boilers when the railways were nationalised in 1948 and No. 46165 *The Ranger (12th London Regt.)* is seen in BR days near Colwyn Bay.

N. Stead

Plate 119 Right No. 6119 *Lancashire Fusilier* passing Carpenders Park in 1933 on an up working of the Royal Train on the occasion of a Royal visit to Liverpool to open the Mersey Tunnel.

C.R.L. Coles

Plate 120 Left The up 'Irish Mail' passing Tring Summit in 1938 behind No. 6127 *Old Contemptibles.*

C.R.L. Coles

Plate 121 Above In 1943 the first of the 'Royal Scots' was fitted by Stanier with the new 2A taper boiler and double chimney. These engines were known officially as 'Converted Royal Scots', although bearing in mind very little of the Fowler engine remained 'Rebuilt Scot' is more appropriate. No. 46144 *Honourable Artillery Company* is seen passing Hatch End on a down Liverpool express in 1949.

C.R.L. Coles

Plate 122 Below No. 46105 *Cameron Highlander* makes a fine sight at Scout Green on the climb to Shap Summit heading a down express.

W. Philip Conolly

Plate 123 Above Smoke deflectors were not fitted immediately after rebuilding but problems with drifting exhaust caused small curved smoke deflectors to be fitted to the entire class from 1947 with the exception of No. 46106 which received straight sided deflectors. No. 46118 *Royal Welch Fusilier* is seen at Hatch End in 1950 on a down Liverpool express.

C.R.L. Coles

Plate 124 Below Converted 'Scots' were extremely successful locomotives and in later years often deputised at short notice for Pacifics. Here the heavy afternoon Euston-Perth, usually Pacific-hauled, is seen on 18th August 1959 leaving Rugby behind No. 46141 *The North Staffordshire Regiment.*

Peter Groom

Plate 125 Above The first of Stanier's Pacifics appeared from Crewe in July 1933, just seventeen months after he had taken office as CME of the LMSR. These supremely handsome four-cylinder engines were designed to replace 'Royal Scots' on the heavy Euston-Glasgow services and a further locomotive was also introduced in 1933, the remaining ten in the class not being delivered until 1935. Here No. 6201 *Princess Elizabeth* nears Carlisle on an up express with its original domeless boiler but with a 4000 gallon, ten ton capacity high curved side tender which was fitted to all twelve of the class late 1936/early 1937.

F.G. Carrier

Plate 126 Below No. 46205 *Princess Victoria* pounding past Harrisons sidings on the climb to Shap Summit with the morning Glasgow-Birmingham train on 19th May 1959.

G.W. Morrison

Plate 127 Left In 1938 No. 6205 *Princess Victoria* is seen heading the up 'Merseyside Express' passing King's Langley. A modified valve motion was fitted to this locomotive in 1937 and the modified bracket can clearly be seen in both this picture and also the picture of No. 46205 on the previous page.

C.R.L. Coles

Plate 128 Right Edge Hill 'Princess Royal' No. 46203 *Princess Margaret Rose* in blue livery heads north past Wembley in 1951 on the down 'Merseyside Express'.

C.R.L. Coles

Plate 129 Below A fine picture of No. 46207 *Princess Arthur of Connaught,* one of the four engines of this class to receive Crimson Lake livery in 1958, leaving Euston on 31st August 1961 heading the down 'Midday Scot'. The entire class had been put into store by early 1961 but some, including No. 46207 were returned to traffic during the summer, only to be put into store again in the autumn. Six engines were rather surprisingly returned to traffic in January 1962 and were finally withdrawn from service in the autumn of 1962.

Peter Groom

Plate 130 Above In June 1935 the sole non-condensing turbine engine was built at Crewe, the Turbomotive as it became known. Although basically similar in many respects to the 'Princess Royal' class, the principle of turbine drive was totally different. There were two turbines at the front of the engine, the large one on the left hand side for forward running and a smaller one on the right hand side for reverse running. During the majority of its life it was employed on Euston-Liverpool services and it is seen here on an up express south of Crewe with its second boiler with steam dome and separate top feed.

F.G. Carrier

Plate 131 Below Although the Turbomotive was given the No. 6202 it was never officially named. It is seen here on 13th August 1949 as BR No. 46202 passing Watford Junction with the 08.30 Euston-Liverpool, having been fitted with smoke deflectors in 1939. When the locomotive required extensive renewals it was decided to rebuild it as a conventional Pacific and she emerged from Crewe in August 1952 as BR No. 46202 *Princess Anne* (see *Plate 267*). Tragically it was damaged beyond economic repair in the Harrow disaster of October 1952.

H.C. Casserley

Plate 132 Above In 1937 five of Stanier's streamlined Pacifics Nos. 6220-6224 were delivered in striking blue livery with silver lining and No. 6223 *Princess Alice* is seen heading the up 'Coronation Scot' near Tamworth. The performance of these outstanding engines was improved still further when they were later fitted with double blast-pipes and chimneys.

F.G. Carrier

Plate 133 Below No. 6231 *Duchess of Atholl* was turned out in 1938 non-streamlined in maroon and gilt livery and it is seen passing Tring Summit on the down 'Midday Scot' shortly after being delivered. This first batch of non-streamlined engines comprised Nos. 6230-6234 and altogether twenty-four engines were constructed in streamlined condition and fourteen engines non-streamlined between 1937 and 1948.

C.R.L. Coles

Plate 134 Right In blue and silver livery the 'Coronation Scot' passing Headstone Lane in 1937 behind No. 6221 *Queen Elizabeth.*
A.G. Ellis Collection

Plate 135 Above No. 6227 *Duchess of Devonshire* was one of the second batch of streamlined engines built in 1938 and is seen in maroon and gold livery coming off the water troughs at Hest Bank on the up 'Royal Scot' in July 1939.
W.H. Foster

Plate 136 Right Maintenance problems aggravated by many inaccessible parts prompted the decision to be taken to remove the streamlined casings from all the locomotives so fitted from 1946. Front end modifications were necessary but the original smokeboxes were retained until they became life expired. As a result the angled smokebox which can be seen in this picture was for sometime a feature of de-streamlined engines. No. 46240 *City of Coventry* recovers from a signal check at Bletchley on the down 'Royal Scot'.
W. Philip Conolly

Plate 137 Above The 'Coronation' Pacifics were all fitted with smoke deflectors after the war and de-streamlined No. 46242 *City of Glasgow* is passing Bay Horse in 1956 on an up express.

W.H. Foster

Plate 138 Below By 1958 de-streamlined No. 46241 *City of Edinburgh* had obtained a new smokebox and it is seen climbing towards Shap Summit at Scout Green on the down 'Royal Scot' on 26th May 1958.

G.W. Morrison

Plate 139 Right No. 46223 *Princess Alice* is still seen with an angled smokebox on 7th May 1950 passing Polmadie on an up express.

J.L. Stevenson

Plate 140 Above No. 46250 *City of Lichfield* was one of the non-streamlined engines built in 1944 and here it is seen leaving Lancaster Castle with a down express. Note the continuation of the footplating at the front end which was a feature of the non-streamlined engines.

British Rail/Oxford Publishing Co.

Plate 141 Right On 12th August 1960 No. 46244 *King George VI* is ready to leave Glasgow Central on the up 'Midday Scot'. It is hard to understand why the last nineteen engines of this fine class, precisely half the entire class of thirty-eight, were so unceremoniously withdrawn in September 1964, only to be replaced by very mediocre diesels, when some of the 'Coronation' Pacifics were reputed to be in such extremely good mechanical condition.

G.W. Morrison

Plate 142 Above The Fowler post-grouping development of the Johnson Midland design was the standard LMS shunting engine. 422 of these 0-6-0Ts were built between 1924 and 1930 and several examples have been preserved. These 3F 0-6-0Ts were nick-named 'Jinties' in later years and No. 47662 is on station pilot duties at Lancaster Castle on 13th May 1964.

M. Welch

Plate 143 Below Class 3F 0-6-0T No. 47410 climbs from the Quay at Holyhead with a train of cattle bound for the cattle dock on the left hand side of the picture on 2nd September 1965.

S.D. Wainwright

Plate 144 Above Thirty-three of these 2-6-0: 0-6-2 Garratts were delivered by Beyer Peacock, the three prototypes in 1927 and the remaining thirty in 1930. No. 4999 was one of the prototypes, Nos. 4997-9, and these first three were the only ones to be fitted with vacuum brakes. They were also fitted with rigid rectangular coal bunkers and No. 4999 worked a test train from Derby to St. Pancras in 1936 with a Dynamometer car next to the engine. It is seen after leaving Derby near Borrowash just before it ran hot and had to be removed from the train.

F.G. Carrier

Plate 145 Below In December 1954 BR No. 47987 is nearing Melton Mowbray with an up freight. The Beyer Peacock patent steam driven rotary coal bunker as fitted in 1932/3 to all but two engines is clearly seen. BR Nos. 47998 and 47999 retained their rigid bunkers and the last of the class, No. 47994 was withdrawn in 1958.

Peter Groom

Plate 146 Above The Stanier 8F 2-8-0 became the standard heavy freight engine of the LMS, 852 being built between 1935 and 1945, many going overseas during World War II. Unusually No. 48553 is seen on passenger duty heading a return excursion from Cleethorpes in May 1959.

N. Stead

Plate 147 Below In 1962 No. 48294 on more customary freight duty is passing Heaton Lodge Junction, Mirfield heading an eastbound fitted freight.

D.I. Wood

Plate 148 Above On 15th February 1962 No. 48532 struggles past Peak Forest summit with a heavy mixed freight from the Manchester area to Buxton. Several of these efficient engines lasted until steam was eliminated from British Rail in 1968 and a few examples have been preserved.

J.S. Whiteley

Plate 149 Below One hundred and seventy-five of these Fowler 7F 0-8-0s were introduced between 1929 and 1932 but were superseded by Stanier's taper-boilered 8Fs. Often referred to as 'Austin Sevens' No. 49578 is leaving Standedge Tunnel near Marsden in 1957 with a train of coal and coke empties. The last member of the class was withdrawn in 1962.

G.W. Morrison

A GLIMPSE AT THE SOMERSET AND DORSET

Plate 150 Left The Somerset and Dorset Joint Railway ran from Bath Junction to Broadstone connecting Bath and Bournemouth via a very scenic line which ran over the Mendip Hills with a summit of 811 feet above sea level at Masbury. The MPD at Bath was not far from the terminus, Bath, Green Park and on shed on Sunday 7th June 1964 are to be seen two classes of engines which gave stirling service to the line. On the left is S & D Class 7F 2-8-0 No. 53807 and on the right Class 4F 0-6-0 No. 44558.

G.W. Morrison

Plate 151 Above On 28th July 1962 S & D 7F 2-8-0 No. 53808 near Wellow on a Nottingham-Birmingham train.

G.W. Morrison

Plate 152 Left A summer Saturdays only Birmingham-Bournemouth train behind 2P 4-4-0 No. 40700 and BR standard Class 5 4-6-0 No. 73087 on 12th August 1961. They are leaving Chilcompton Tunnel working hard on the severe climb from Radstock to Masbury Summit.

G.W. Morrison

Plate 153 Right The severe climb to Masbury Summit started at Evercreech Junction and many northbound trains were assisted from here for the climb over the Mendips. Class 2P 4-4-0 No. 40564 and 7F 2-8-0 No. 53806 are leaving Evercreech Junction on 9th September 1961 on a Bournemouth-Nottingham train. The mechanical tablet catching apparatus for single line working can be seen behind the cab of the 2P.

G.W. Morrison

Plate 154 Below Nos. 40564 and 53806 are seen again on the same train working hard on the 1 in 50 gradient at the approach to Winsor Hill Tunnel about two miles from Masbury Summit.

G.W. Morrison

TITLED TRAINS

Plate 155 Left The name 'Royal Scot' was given to the 10.00 departures from Euston and Glasgow Central in 1927 and during its career has incorporated stops at Rugby, Crewe, Preston, Carlisle and Symington with additional stops during part of the War. In this 1955 picture 'Coronation 4-6-2 No. 46238 *City of Carlisle* make an impressive sight restarting from Carlisle on the up train.

I.S. Carr

Plate 156 Below De-streamlined Pacific No. 46220 *Coronation* is passing through Crewe, also on the u train.

T. Lewis

Plate 157 Above Prior to 1927 the 'Mid-Day Scot' was known as 'The Corridor' as it was one of the first LNWR expresses to be formed of entirely corridor stock. On 21st May 1956 the 'Mid-Day Scot' is seen leaving Euston at 13.15 on its eight hour and twenty minutes journey to Glasgow Central behind 'Coronation' Pacific No. 46233 *Duchess of Sutherland.*

Peter Groom

Plate 158 Below The down train is seen again, this time behind 'Princess Royal' Pacific No. 46212 *Duchess of Kent,* restarting from its Rugby stop on 24th July 1958.

Peter Groom

Plate 159 Left The 'Coronation Scot' began running in summer 1937 between Euston and Glasgow with one intermediate stop at Carlisle, leaving both Euston and Glasgow Central at 13.30. No. 6220 *Coronation* is heading the up train near Tamworth.

F.G. Carrier

Plate 160 Above The 'Caledonian' was only introduced in 1959 and 'Coronation' Pacific No. 46240 *City of Coventry* is seen leaving Glasgow Central on 21st July 1959 at 08.30 on the up train. In 1962 both the up and down trains were retimed including additional stops and the title disappeared in Autumn 1964.

G.W. Morrison

Plate 161 Above When the 'Comet' first received its name in 1932 it left Manchester London Road station at 17.40 and Euston at 11.50. Over the years various alterations were made and in summer 1954 it had been retimed to leave Euston at 09.45, with stops at Stoke-on-Trent, Macclesfield and Stockport, and to leave Manchester at 17.50 with an arrival of 21.20 at Euston. Here the down train is seen on 26th November 1951 passing Heaton Norris behind converted 'Scot' No. 46160 *Queen Victoria's Rifleman.*

T. Lewis

Plate 162 Right The 'Mancunian' also ran between Euston and Manchester London Road and the up train is seen near Cheadle Hulme behind Stanier Class 5 4-6-0 No. 44750 fitted with Caprotti valve gear.

T. Lewis

Plate 163 Above In the late 1950's the up 'Mancunian' is running into Euston past the customary collection of spotters behind Longsight 'Scot' No. 46160 *Queen Victoria's Rifleman.*

M. Welch

Plate 164 Below The 'Palatine' ran between St. Pancras and Manchester Central via the Midland route and the name was revived in 1957. Here Kentish Town converted 'Scot' is about to leave St. Pancras at 07.55 on the down train on 9th April 1958.

J.D. Edwards

Plate 165 Above The 'Red Rose' began running in 1951 as the 12.05 ex Euston and the 17.25 ex Liverpool Lime Street. Later in 1951 it was retimed to 12.30 ex Euston with a three and three quarter hour non-stop run to Lime Street. Here 'Princess Royal' pacific No. 46204 *Princess Louise* passes a crowd of spotters at Crewe on 28th March 1959 on the down train.

S.D. Wainwright

Plate 166 Right In 1951 the down 'Merseyside Express' which left Euston for Liverpool Lime Street at 18.05 is seen tearing through Harrow and Wealdstone behind Edge Hill Pacific No. 46200 *The Princess Royal*. The only intermediate stop was at Edge Hill to detach the Southport portion and Lime Street was reached at 21.50.

C.R.L. Coles

Plate 167 Above In 1954 the 16.30 Euston-Liverpool Lime Street was retimed to depart Euston at 16.55 and given the name the 'Shamrock'. It is seen here at Euston on 14th June 1954 about to leave on its inaugural non-stop run behind converted 'Scot' No. 46153 *The Royal Dragoon,* arriving at Lime Street at 20.22.

B. Morrison

Plate 168 Left The up 'Shamrock' left Liverpool Lime Street at 08.10, and with only one intermediate stop at Bletchley was due into Euston at 11.45. However, during the electrification period there were severa timetable alterations and it is seen at 12.34 after arrival at Euston behind a rathe dirty 'Princess Royal' Pacific No. 46211 *Queen Maud.*

W. Philip Conoll

Plate 169 Right In 1957 the title of the 'Waverley' was given to the 09.15 St. Pancras-Edinburgh Waverley replacing the title of the 'Thames-Forth Express' which the train had carried from 1927 until the outbreak of war. The train ran via Nottingham, Leeds, Carlisle and via the Waverley route to Edinburgh and it is seen ready to leave St. Pancras in 1959 with Midland 2P 4-4-0 No. 40421 piloting an unidentified 'Jubilee' 4-6-0.

M. Welch

Plate 170 Left The morning train in each direction between St. Pancras and Glasgow was given the title the 'Thames-Clyde Express' in 1927, regaining it after the War in 1949. The route was via Leicester, Leeds, Carlisle and the Glasgow and South Western Line to Glasgow St. Enoch. On 21st February 1960 Holbeck 'Jubilee' No. 45564 *New South Wales* is preparing to leave Leeds City, after reversal, on the down train.

G.W. Morrison

FREIGHT TRAFFIC

Plate 171 Above Kirtley Midland double framed 1F 0-6-0 No. 2498 on a down rake of empties near Peckwash Mill Sidings, between Derby and Duffield.

F.G. Carrier

Plate 172 Left One of the ten Maryport and Carlisle 2F 0-6-0s No. 12488 leaving Carlisle northbound on a mixed freight in the late 1920s. The last of these 5 ft 1½ in engines was withdrawn in 1930.

A.G. Ellis Collection

Plate 173 Above Pride of the LNWR express passenger engines on a class 'A' freight. Reboilered 'Claughton' No. 6017 *Breadalbane* heading a Camden-Walsall freight passing Headstone Lane in 1938.
C.R.L. Coles

Plate 174 Left The London Tilbury and Southend Railway only possessed two 0-6-0s which were built in 1899. No. 2898 which was withdrawn in 1933 heads an up freight.
A.G. Ellis Collection

Plate 175 Right On 8th October 1930 Hughes L & YR 6F 0-8-0 No. 12826 leaves Agecroft for Gorton towing Beyer-Peacock Garratt No. 4972 which had not yet been officially handed over to the LMS from the builders, Beyer-Peacock. Representatives of the big four railways had been displayed at Wavertree playing fields, Liverpool, on the occasion of the Liverpool & Manchester Railway Centenary and then stabled at Agecroft before being dispersed.
A.G. Ellis Collection

Plate 176 Left An impressive picture of Beyer-Garratt 2-6-0: 0-6-2 No. 47969 recovering from a signal check at Stamford with a freight for Peterborough on 4th January 1952.
P.H. Wells

Plate 177 Below LMS built 4F 0-6-0 No. 44459 accelerates a heavy southbound ore train through the beautiful Lune gorge.
British Rail/Oxford Publishing Co.

Plate 178 Above On 15th March 1959 Class 3F 0-6-0T No. 47297 is shunting in the yard at Chester, adjacent to Chester General station.

S.D. Wainwright

Plate 179 Below Class 8F 2-8-0 No. 48448 struggles up the last few yards to Copy Pit Summit between Burnley and Todmorden on 6th April 1968 heading a Wyre Dock-Healey Mills coal empties.

J.S. Whiteley

Plate 180 Above Unrebuilt 'Patriots' were frequently seen on both freight and parcels traffic and No. 45506 *The Royal Pioneer Corps* is leaving the picturesque station of Colwyn Bay on 1st September 1953 heading an up parcels.
R.E. Vincent

Plate 181 Below Only in their latter years were the rebuilt 'Patriots' to be seen regularly on freight workings and on a stormy August day in 1964 No. 45531 *Sir Frederick Harrison* is climbing Shap with banking assistance on a down freight.
M. Welch

Plate 182 Right Class 7F 0-8-0 of LNW design No. 49078 is seen in West London passing Kensington Olympia on 18th June 1955.
A.G. Ellis Collection

Plate 183 Left Freight of a slightly different kind, to be more precise, the Horwich works shunter on 9th August 1953. Eight of these 18 in gauge 0-4-0STs were built 1887/1901 for shunting at the L & YR works. *Wren* was the last working locomotive of the class surviving until 1962 and can now be seen preserved at the York National Railway Museum.
A.G. Ellis Collection

Plate 184 Right Jack of all trades; Class 5 4-6-0 No. 45024 recovering from a cruel signal check on the climb to Shap Summit near Thrimby Grange on 13th April 1963 heading a heavy southbound freight.
J.S. Whiteley

Plate 185 Above 'Jubilee' class 4-6-0 No. 45581 *Bihar and Orissa* heading a short westbound parcels passes Class 3F 0-6-0T No. 47379 on shunting duties just outside Batley. 18th July 1962.

D.I. Wood

Plate 186 Below Many of the last surviving 8F 2-8-0s ended their days in the Buxton area and on 15th February 1968 No. 48191 passes Peak Forest Summit with a local freight from Buxton.

J.S. Whiteley

Plate 187 Above Two 4-4-0s passing non-stop through Duffield make a superb sight heading a down express. Midland 6 ft 9 in 2P No. 338 is piloting LMS 6 ft 9 in Compound No. 1050.
F.G. Carrier

DOUBLE-HEADED TRAINS

Plate 188 Below A 'Claughton' 4-6-0 and a 2P 4-4-0 are double-heading a down train near Breadsall Crossing in the mid 1930s.
F.G. Carrier

Plate 189 Above Two Kirtley Midland double-framed 1F 0-6-0s, the leading one No. 2430, both with Salter spring balance safety valves, head a down mixed freight near Peckwash Mill sidings.

F.G. Carrier

Plate 190 Below In August 1934 Johnson Midland 1P 2-4-0 No. 213 is piloting an unidentified Midland 4F near Bell Busk on a Skipton-Carnforth train.

W.H. Foster

Plate 191 Left On the Highland main line a 'Small Ben' 4-4-0 is piloting a 'Castle' 4-6-0 on a southbound train in the mid 1930s.

F.G. Carrier

Plate 192 Below Double-heading northbound from Carlisle was often the order of the day before the 4-6-0s were introduced and in this picture 'Dunalastair IV' 4-4-0 No. 14358 is piloting LMS built three cylinder compound No. 1066 on a down express leaving Carlisle.

A.G. Ellis Collection

Plate 193 Left An unusual pairing at Mill Hill in 1923; Whitelegg London Tilbury & Southend 'Baltic' tank No. 2106 paired with Midland '483' class 4-4-0 No. 555 provide super power for a down St. Albans train.

A.G. Ellis Collection

Plate 194 Above On 21st May 1955 Midland 2P 4-4-0 No. 40556 is piloting BR standard Class 2 2-6-0 No. 78023 away from Dore and Totley on an up Sheffield local.

B.R. Goodlad

Plate 195 Below An impressive combination of LNWR and LMS engines on an up express near Tamworth. A 'Claughton' 4-6-0 is coupled in front of a 'Royal Scot' 4-6-0 which has been fitted with the first type of straight sided smoke deflectors.

F.G. Carrier

Plate 196 Above A fine picture of Rugby 6 ft 9 in 'Precedent' class 2-4-0 No. 5011 *Director* piloting a reboilered 'Claughton' near Tamworth on a down express.

F.G. Carrier

Plate 197 Right Whale LNWR 'Precursor' 4-4-0 No. 5295 *Scorpion* is picking up on Brock troughs, between Preston and Lancaster, whilst piloting a 'Claughton' 4-6-0 on a heavy down express.

A.G. Ellis Collection

Plate 198 Left LNWR 'George the Fifth' class 4-4-0 with its 1934 number 25393 *Loyalty* is restarting a down Bletchley train from Harrow and Wealdstone whilst piloting an LMS 2-6-4T in the mid 1930s.
C.R.L. Coles

Plate 199 Above In the autumn of 1938, Midland 2P 4-4-0 No. 489 is piloting 'Jubilee' class 4-6-0 No. 5621 *Northern Rhodesia* near Cotehill, on an up express, attached for the severe climb to Ais Gill Summit on its journey to Leeds and the south.
E.E. Smith

Plate 200 Left It was very unusual to see a 4-4-0 piloting a Pacific but on 7th August 1958 2P No. 40679 was paired at Crewe with 'Coronation' No. 46228 *Duchess of Rutland* on the nineteen coach down 'Mid-Day Scot'. In all probability the Pacific would be pushing the 4-4-0 as well as pulling the train for most of the journey!
S.D. Wainwright

Plate 201 Above Double-heading was common between Manchester and Leeds for the climb over the Pennines with the summit at Standedge Tunnel. On 12th May 1956 LMS 2P 4-4-0 No. 40587 and 'Jubilee' 4-6-0 No. 45646 *Napier* are passing Heaton Lodge Junction, Mirfield on the morning Liverpool-Newcastle.

B.R. Goodlad

Plate 202 Below The Euston-Perth trains were often worked by Pacifics but on 9th August 1960 Stanier Class 5 4-6-0 No. 45174 and 'Jubilee' class 4-6-0 No. 45729 *Furious* double-head the down morning train out of Carlisle near Kingmoor MPD.

G.W. Morrison

Plate 203 Above LMS and LNER motive power combined on the Heaton-Manchester Red Bank empty vans passing York MPD on 22nd August 1959. Class 4F 0-6-0 No. 44207 is piloting LNER Class J39 0-6-0 No. 64824.

N. Stead

Plate 204 Below Another picture of the Heaton-Red Bank vans, this time in the Calder Valley on Luddendenfoot troughs. Hughes/Fowler 'Crab' 2-6-0 No. 42701 is piloting a Stanier Class 5 4-6-0, both picking up water before the westbound climb to Summit Tunnel followed by the long descent to Manchester.

G.W. Morrison

Plate 205 Right The peace of the desolate fells near Shap Summit is disturbed by Fairburn 2-6-4T No. 42198 and Stanier Class 5 4-6-0 No. 45218 battling up the last mile of 1 in 75 heading the Sunday 13.05 Manchester and Liverpool-Glasgow and Edinburgh on 28th June 1964.

J.S. Whiteley

Plate 206 Left Between intermittent snow showers on a bitterly cold day in April 1964 Fairburn 2-6-4T No. 42110 pilots 'Royal Scot' No. 46162 *Queen's Westminster Rifleman* on a Crewe-Carlisle parcels. The tank engine was attached at Oxenholme and will pilot the 'Scot' to Shap Summit. The pair are seen on Dillicar Troughs, Tebay, taking a run at the climb from Tebay to Shap Summit.

J. S. Whiteley

late 207 Right On 12th July 964 Stanier 2-6-4T No. 42449 nd rebuilt 'Patriot' 4-6-0 No. 5512 *Bunsen* are nearing Shap ummit on the Sunday 09.30 lanchester-Glasgow and Edinurgh. On Sundays at this eriod, Tebay shed was closed nd any train wanting assistance ook a pilot from Oxenholme.

J.S. Whiteley

Plate 208 Above A pair of Stanier Class 5s, Nos. 44956 and 44973 are leaving Arrochar on 13th August 1960 heading the 06.30 Mallaig-Glasgow Queen Street.

G.W. Morrison

Plate 209 Below Stanier Class 5 4-6-0s Nos. 44973 and 44975 are climbing the 1 in 45 from Glasgow Queen Street to Cowlairs on the 10.15 to Fort William on 12th August 1960.

G.W. Morrison

SHED SCENES

Plate 210 Right Holbeck, Leeds on 17th March 1963. One of the roundhouses can be seen on the left and the Manchester line on the viaduct in the background.
J.S. Whiteley

Plate 211 Below Inside Holbeck in July 1967.
J.S. Whiteley

Plate 212 Above In the yard at Carlisle Upperby on 22nd May 1961. 'Jubilee' No. 45700 *Amethyst* and 'Coronation' No. 46248 *City of Leeds* are in the foreground.

G.W. Morrison

Plate 213 Below Super power inside Crewe North on 26th February 1961 in the shape of three 'Coronation' Pacifics and Polmadie 'Royal Scot'.

S.D. Wainwright

Plate 214 Left A mixture of Midland and Lancashire & Yorkshire designs at Manningham on 23rd March 1952.
B.R. Goodlad

Plate 215 Left Four of the total class of ten L & YR 'Baltic' tanks, at Agecroft.
A.G. Ellis Collection

Plate 216 Below In the yard at Springs Branch (Wigan) on 26th August 1955. Aspinall L & YR Class F19 0-6-0 as BR No. 52341 appears to have recently had a new smokebox fitted.
B. Morrison

Plate 217 *Above* Both these locomotives have just had their smokeboxes cleaned out at Camden on 5th June 1960.
Peter Groom

Plate 218 *Below* An unusual visitor to St. Rollox in the shape of a 'Coronation' Pacific, there because of diversions from Glasgow Central on 12th April 1959.
G.W. Morrison

Plate 219 Top Shap bankers at Tebay on 16th August 1958.
G.W. Morrison

Plate 220 Centre Beattock shed on 20th May 1961.
G.W. Morrison

Plate 221 Right Some of the last Stanier 8F 2-8-0s at Rose Grove on 17th February 1968, only a few months before BR withdrew the last steam locomotives from service.
G.W. Morrison

FAMOUS MAIN LINE INCLINES

SHAP

Plate 222 Above Shap Summit a
914 feet above sea level on the
West Coast main line is the culm
ation of almost thirty-two miles
of steady climbing for northbou
trains from Carnforth which is
only just above sea level. Heavy
down trains often took banking
assistance from Tebay for the
final five and three quarter miles
to the summit which is mainly a
1 in 75. Southbound trains are a
faced with about thirty-two mil
of uphill work, from Carlisle, bu
the final climb to Shap Summit
not quite as severe as for north-
bound trains. On 17th July 196
Class 8F 2-8-0 No. 48730 is seen
passing Shap Wells on a down
freight with a Fowler 2-6-4T
working equally hard at the rear
J.S. Whitele

Plate 223 Below Having taken a run at the final 1 in 75 through the Lune Gorge from Grayrigg, 'Coronation' Pacific No. 46225 *Duchess of Gloucester* roars past Greenholme just north of Tebay on a lightweight down express on 29th April 1963.

J.S. Whiteley

Plate 224 Above On Whit Sunday, 10th June 1962 No. 46252 *City of Leicester* makes a splendid sight climbing through the woods near Little Strickland heading the up 'Royal Scot' combined with the relief, probably because of engine failure, a fifteen coach train.

J.S. Whiteley

Plate 225 Below For up trains the final thirteen miles from Penrith to the summit is predominantly at 1 in 125 and No. 46243 *City of Lancaster* is nearing Shap village on 29th August 1959 on the up 'Royal Scot'.

G.W. Morrison

THE LICKEY INCLINE

Plate 226 Left On the Midland line from Gloucester to Birmingham northbound trains are faced with slightly more than two miles at 1 in 37¾ from Bromsgrove to Blackwell. Most trains took banking assistance and on 7th July 1956 Midland 2P 4-4-0 No. 40486 comes slowly up the gradient with a Gloucester-Birmingham stopping train.

G.W. Morrison

BEATTOCK

Plate 227 Right The other notorious climb on the West Coast main line is between Carlisle and Glasgow and Beattock Summit at 1015 feet above sea level is almost exactly half way between the two cities. The north-bound climb is the most severe with virtually ten miles between 1 in 88 and 1 in 69 from Beattock station to the summit. Most north-bound trains took banking assistance for the climb and Stanier Class 5 4-6-0 No. 45485 is nearing Greskine on 23rd April 1962 with a down freight.

J.S. Whiteley

Plate 228 Above 'Royal Scot' class 4-6-0 No. 46107 *Argyll and Sutherland Highlander* is working hard with a full head of steam on the 09.30 Manchester-Glasgow passing Harthope on 23rd April 1962.

J.S. Whiteley

Plate 229 Below 'Jubilee' class 4-6-0 No. 45602 *British Honduras* is also seen near Harthope on the last lap of the climb to the summit on the morning Liverpool-Glasgow on 23rd April 1962.

J.S. Whiteley

Plate 230 Above The southbound climb to Beattock Summit is far more leisurely with just a gentle climb up the Clyde Valley from Carstairs to Crawford and a final two and a quarter miles at 1 in 99 from Elvanfoot to the summit. Pacific No. 46256 *Sir William A. Stanier, F.R.S.* is near Crawford on the 09.00 Perth-Euston on 15th April 1963.

J.S. Whiteley

Plate 231 Below Just out of Euston, down trains face a sharp climb of almost one mile at between 1 in 70 and 1 in 112 to Camden No. 1. This often proved tricky for cold engines and rebuilt 'Royal Scot' 4-6-0 No. 46157 *The Royal Artilleryma* is seen with sanders on heading an afternoon Liverpool express in October 1956.

Peter Groo

Plate 232 Above En route from Carnforth to Shap Summit, between Crewe and Carlisle, the first prolonged stiff climb facing northbound trains is the thirteen miles from near Milnthorpe to the intermediate summit at Grayrigg. The last seven miles from Oxenholme steepen to between 1 in 104 and 1 in 131 and converted 'Royal Scot' No. 46107 *Argyll and Sutherland Highlander* with the help of banking assistance from Oxenholme is heading a Manchester-Glasgow in April 1954.

W.H. Foster

GRAYRIGG

Plate 233 Below Earlier in the day, at the same location near Lambrigg Crossing, Carlisle Kingmoor unrebuilt 'Patriot' 4-6-0 No. 45549 climbs towards Grayrigg with a Crewe-Carlisle parcels.

W.H. Foster

AIS GILL AND BLEA MOOR

Plate 234 Above Without doubt one of the most spectacular railway lines in Britain is the Settle and Carlisle section of the Midland route from Leeds to Carlisle. It crosses the backbone of England in a most breathtaking manner with the help of some superb feats of railway engineering which claimed many lives during construction between 1869 and 1875. The summit of the line is at Ais Gill, 1169 feet above sea level in bleak and windswept Fells, about sixty-four miles from Leeds and forty-eight miles from Carlisle. 'Jubilee' class 4-6-0 No. 45597 *Barbados* is crossing the 440 yard long Batty Moss viaduct at Ribblehead heading the down 'Waverley' on 3rd October 1959, nearing the top of the fourteen and a half mile climb at mainly 1 in 100 from Settle Junction to Blea Moor Tunnel.

G.W. Morrison

Plate 235 Above Between Blea Moor and Ais Gill the railway hugs the 1150 feet contour for about eleven miles and Class 5 4-6-0 No. 45254 approaches the summit at Ais Gill on a southbourn freight, having almost completed the fifteen and a half mile climb at mainly 1 in 100 from Ormside viaduct, just south of Appleby on 30th April 1966.

J.S. Whiteley

LOCOMOTIVE PORTRAITS

MIDLAND

Plate 236 Left Kirtley double framed 1P 2-4-0 No. 20012 as renumbered in 1934. Twenty-nine of these engines were built between 1866 and 1874, the last one being withdrawn in 1947.
F.G. Carrier

Plate 237 Right Johnson '483' class 4-4-0 as fitted with bogie brakes.
F.G. Carrier

Plate 238 Left Johnson 3P 4-4-0 as rebuilt by Fowler.
F.G. Carrier

Plate 239 Right Johnson 3F 0-6-0 No. 3826. The beaded splashers can clearly be seen in this picture.
F.G. Carrier

LONDON AND NORTH WESTERN

Plate 240 Right Whale rebuilt 'Precursor' No. 25298 *Dragon* at Peterborough on 29th August 1936. One hundred and thirty of these 4-4-0s were built between 1904 and 1907 but only one survived nationalisation and was withdrawn later in 1948.

A.G. Ellis Collection

Plate 241 Left Bowen-Cooke 'Prince of Wales' Class 3P No. 25631 *Felicia Hemans.*

F.G. Carrier

NORTH LONDON

Plate 242 Right Sharp Stewart crane engine built in 1858 as 0-4-0ST but rebuilt as 0-4-2ST in 1872 and crane fitted. It was BR No. 58865 and was withdrawn in 1951 after being a permanent shunter at Bow Works.

F.G. Carrier

Plate 243 Left J.C. Park 1F 0-6-0T No. 58857 at Poplar Dock on 5th May 1956. Thirty of these were built between 1887 and 1905 and this engine was formerly NLR No. 18, LNWR No. 2878 and LMS No. 7517.

R.E. Vincent

LONDON AND NORTH WESTERN

Plate 244 Left BR No. 58926 at Crewe Works in May 1959, the last surviving Webb 'coal tank'. Three hundred of these engines were built between 1881 and 1896.

N. Stead

Plate 245 Right Beames 5F 0-8-4T No. 7953. Thirty of these engines were built but were not delivered until after the grouping, between 1923 and 1924.

A.G. Ellis Collection

FURNESS

Plate 246 Left Rutherford 3P 4-6-4T No.11103. Only five of these massive engines were built in 1921 and lasted until 1940.

A.G. Ellis Collection

Plate 247 Right Pettigrew 3F 0-6-0 seen as BR No. 52494. Nineteen of these engines were built between 1913 and 1920, six survived nationalisation, the last one being withdrawn in 1957.

N. Stead

LANCASHIRE & YORKSHIRE

Plate 248 Above Hughes 5P 4-6-0 No. 10456 as rebuilt as a compound in 1926. It is seen at Upperby shed on 16th July 1933. A total of seventy of these superheated four cylinder 'Lanky Bombers' were built between 1921 and 1925 (L & YR class N1), fifteen of which were rebuilt from the original saturated design of 1908.

F.G. Carrier

Plate 249 Right Aspinall 6F 0-8-0 No. 12753 which was built at Horwich in 1907 and withdrawn in March 1939.

N. Stead

HIGHLAND

Plate 250 Left Jones 'Loch' 2P 4-4-0 No. 14379 *Loch Insh* built in 1896. Eighteen of these engines were built, fifteen in 1896 and three in 1917. No. 14379 was one of several rebuilt with larger CR type boilers as seen here at Aviemore in 1948.

F.G. Carrier

Plate 251 Left Drummond 'Small Ben' 2P 4-4-0 as BR No. 54398 *Ben Alder.* Twenty 'Small Bens' were built between 1898 and 1906, all eventually acquiring CR type boilers.

N. Stead

Plate 252 Right Smith 'River' Class 4P 4-6-0 No. 14761 at Perth MPD. This was one of six engines built for the Highland but subsequently sold to the CR after being found too heavy for the lines of the HR.

T.G. Hepburn

CALEDONIAN

Plate 253 Left The sole 7ft 0in Neilson & Co. 1P 4-2-2 built in 1886. This engine has been restored as original CR No. 123 but is seen on 17th April 1933 at Perth.

F.G. Carrier

Plate 254 Right McIntosh 'Dunalastair II Rebuilt' 3P 4-4-0 No. 14432 at Stirling. Only four of this class were built in 1898 and were rebuilt in 1914 with superheated boiler.

T.G. Hepburn

Plate 255 Left McIntosh '139' class 3P 4-4-0 No. 14443 at Kingmoor. Twenty-two of these 6 ft 6 in engines were built between 1910-14, the last one surviving until 1957.
T.G. Hepbu

Plate 256 Right One of the two D. Drummond unclassified 'Killin Tanks' built at St. Rollox in 1885. These engines worked the Killin branch until 1895 when they were replaced by 0-4-4Ts. No. 15001 is at Inverness on 16th April 1933.
F.G. Carrier

Plate 257 Left McIntosh '34' class 3F 2-6-0 No. 17801 at Perth on 21st May 1934. Only five of these were built in 1912 and they were withdrawn between 1935 and 1937.
F.G. Carrier

Plate 258 Right Eleven of these handsome McIntosh '179' class 4-6-0s were built between 1913-14, the last one surviving until 1946. No. 17913 is at Perth on 21st May 1934.
F.G. Carrier